HISPANIC HOLIDAYS

by Faith Winchester

Reading Consultant:
Gerald J. Mac Donald

Bridgestone Books

an Imprint of Capstone Press

Fast Facts

• Hispanics are the fastest growing ethnic group in the United States.

• Hispanics make up 10 percent of the population of the United States.

• Many Hispanics live in California, Texas, and Florida.

• Almost all Hispanics are Roman Catholic.

Bridgestone Books are published by Capstone Press • 818 North Willow Street, Mankato, Minnesota 56001
Copyright © 1996 by Capstone Press • All rights reserved • Printed in the United States of America

Library of Congress Cataloging-in-Publication Data
Winchester, Faith.
   Hispanic Holidays/by Faith Winchester.
   p. cm.--(Read-and-discover ethnic holidays)
   Includes bibliographical references and index.
   Summary: Briefly introduces Hispanic Americans and discusses eight Hispanic holidays. Includes instructions for making confetti-filled eggs.
   ISBN 1-56065-457-0
   1. Holidays--Latin America--Juvenile literature. 2. Latin Americans--Social life and customs--Juvenile literature. 3. Hispanic Americans--Social life and custom--Juvenile literature. [1. Holidays--Latin America. 2. Hispanic Americans--Social life and customs.] I. Title. II. Series.
GT 4813.5.A2W55 1996
394.2'698--dc20
                              96-25912
                                 CIP
                                 AC

Photo credits
Bob Daemmrich, cover. International Stock, 4, 6, 10, 14.
FPG, 8, 16, 20. Unicorn/Alon Reininger, 12. Beryl Goldberg, 18.

Table of Contents

Words in **boldface** type in the text are defined in the Words to Know section in the back of this book.

Hispanics

Hispanics are people who speak Spanish or have Spanish-speaking **ancestors**. They come from many different countries. Many are from Mexico and Latin America. The United States has more Hispanic **immigrants** than any other ethnic group.

Spanish is the third most used language in the world. Only Mandarin Chinese and English are used more. Many Hispanics speak both English and Spanish. This is called being bilingual. Many people study Spanish because they want to communicate with more people.

Hispanics have a rich history. Their culture and background are important. They keep many of the traditions and holidays of their homelands.

Hispanic celebrations are often called fiestas. This is a Spanish word meaning festival or party. Fiestas are an important part of Hispanic life. They remind Hispanics of their culture.

Hispanic celebrations are called fiestas.

Cinco de Mayo

Cinco de Mayo is Spanish for the fifth of May. This holiday celebrates the Mexican army's victory over the French. The battle took place in 1862 in the Mexican town of Puebla. The Mexican army was very small and unprepared. But the men were brave.

Benito Juarez led the army that defeated the French. He was a great leader. The Mexican people respected him. This battle was an important battle to win. It gave Mexico more freedom.

Today, Hispanics remember Cinco de Mayo. It is a happy time. Men dress up as soldiers and pretend to have a fight. Mexico always wins over the French in these make-believe wars.

Some Hispanic communities have parades. People decorate floats with many flowers. Everyone dresses up. They eat Mexican food. Many people who are not Hispanic celebrate and eat Mexican food that day, too. A display of fireworks ends the day.

Cinco de Mayo is celebrated with parades and fireworks.

Easter Season

The Easter season begins in February or March. It is a holiday that all Christians celebrate. Lent begins 40 days before Easter. During Lent, people decide to do something that is not easy for them. They do this to show devotion to God.

Holy Week is the week before Easter. Thursday of Holy Week is set aside to remember the Last Supper Jesus had with his apostles. On Friday, Jesus' death on the cross is remembered. Easter Sunday is a happy day. It is the day Christians believe Jesus rose from the dead.

Many people go to church on Easter morning. Then, they return home for a big dinner. After dinner, children look for decorated Easter eggs. They have fights with cascarones. These are real eggshells filled with confetti. Children throw the cascarones at each other. The eggs break and the confetti bursts out. Easter is both fun and **solemn**.

Easter remembers Jesus' death on the cross and resurrection.

Corpus Christi

Corpus Christi takes place on the eighth Thursday after Easter. It is a religious holiday. The purpose of the holiday is to remember and celebrate the importance of Holy Communion. During Communion, Christians remember the Last Supper. Jesus predicted his death at the supper.

Many Hispanics go to the Mass of Corpus Christi. It is usually on a Sunday. They sing and have a procession. It is like a religious parade. The religious leaders and the important people of the community lead the procession. They carry bread and wine. Sometimes the path of the procession is decorated with flowers.

Everyone returns to the church to hear the benediction. This is a short blessing at the end of a worship service. After the service, people have dinner with their families. Sometimes they celebrate the holiday with a dance after dinner.

Hispanics sing and dance during Corpus Christi.

Saint John's Day

Saint John the Baptist is the patron saint of water. A patron saint watches over a certain thing. Saint John the Baptist is said to be the keeper of water because he baptized many people. Catholics believe baptism cleanses them of sin.

Hispanics remember Saint John the Baptist on June 24. It is called Saint John's Day or San Juan's Day. It is a day to celebrate water. Wells, fountains, and pools are decorated with candles and flowers. Parties are held along the shores of rivers and lakes. Flowers are sent floating on the water.

Children celebrate this holiday by pushing each other into the water. No one wears very nice clothes that day because they know they will get wet. The holiday is not complete unless they are thrown into a pool at least once.

This day is also called Bath Day. It is the day when the statues of the saints get their yearly bath.

Some Hispanics believe if it rains on Saint John's Day, the saint is blessing them.

Day of the Dead

Day of the Dead is one of the most important Hispanic holidays. It takes place on November 1 and 2. It honors friends and relatives who have died during the year. They believe the dead come to share a feast with the living. It is a happy time.

An **altar** is set up in the living room to greet the dead. It holds familiar things. There may be pictures, a favorite article of clothing or food.

On the first day, Hispanics clean the graves. They leave flowers and candles on them. They make white masks to wear. On the second day, there is a procession to the cemetery. They pray for the dead. Sometimes this is sad. They put marigold flowers on the graves. The strong smell will help the dead find their graves again after the feast.

Everything is decorated with skulls, coffins, and skeletons. A special feast is eaten at the graves. Dessert is a sugar bread in the shape of a skull.

The Day of the Dead altar holds special things for the dead.

Posados

Posados is celebrated on the nine nights before Christmas. It begins December 16th. Posada means inn or place to stay. Children act out the story of Jesus' birth. In the Bible story, Mary and Joseph could not find an inn. They stayed in a stable. Jesus was born there and laid in a **manger**.

Each night of Posados, children go from house to house looking for a posada. When they come to the house picked for that night, there is a big party. It is at a different house each night. There is music and games. Sometimes there is a piñata. This is made of paper and paste. It is filled with candy. Blindfolded children try to hit it with a stick to break it open and get the candy. It is a lot of fun.

People decorate with manger scenes and say "Feliz Navidad." This means Merry Christmas in Spanish. Posados is the celebration that begins the Christmas season.

There is a big party on each night of Posados.

Three Kings' Day

Many Hispanics celebrate Three Kings' Day. It is on January 6. It is like celebrating another Christmas. Sometimes this holiday is called Little Christmas. It can also be called Epiphany. It celebrates the Bible story of the three kings who gave gifts to Jesus. It is the end of Christmas.

The three kings are similar to Santa Claus. They bring gifts. Sometimes children even tell the three kings what they want. The night before Three Kings' Day, children put boxes outside their doors. The boxes are filled with grass for the kings' camels. In the morning, the grass is gone. There are gifts instead. It is like Christmas all over again.

Families have a big dinner. One of the most important parts of the dinner is a cake. It is in the shape of a crown. It is decorated with cherries and pineapple. They look like jewels. Three Kings' Day is the first happy celebration of the new year.

Three Kings' Day is sometimes called Little Christmas.

Our Lady of Guadalupe Day

December 12th is the Day of Our Lady of Guadalupe. She is the patron saint of Mexico.

Many Mexican-Americans make a trip to Mexico for the holiday. They go once in their lives. They visit her shrine. It is in the village of Guadalupe, now part of Mexico City.

This holiday is based on an old Mexican story. In 1531, a man named Juan Diego was on Tepeyec Hill. He saw a vision of the Lady. She told him to build a shrine on the hill for her. He had the same vision three times, but no one believed his story.

The Lady gave him a sign to show the people. She told him about a rose bush growing on the hill. He gathered the roses in his coat and ran to show the church leader. When Diego opened his coat, there was a picture of the Lady.

The shrine was built. It is a holy place. The picture and Diego's coat still hang there.

Mexican Americans travel to the shrine of Our Lady of Guadalupe.

Hands On: Make Confetti Eggs

Hispanics make special Easter eggs called cascarones. They are eggshells filled with confetti. You can make cascarones and have your own confetti battle with your friends.

You will need
- eggs
- bowl
- stickers, tape, or flour and water
- needle
- confetti

1. Use a needle to poke a hole in one end of an egg. Keep making the hole bigger until it is a little smaller than a dime.
2. Drain the insides of the egg into a bowl. You can use them later to make eggnog or scrambled eggs.
3. Rinse the eggshells out with water and let them dry.
4. Fill the shells with small, colorful confetti. You can buy it from the store or make it yourself by cutting paper into tiny pieces.
5. Cover the hole with a sticker or some tape. You can also cover the hole with a paste made from flour and water. When it dries, it will be hard but fragile like the shell.
6. Decorate your eggs however you like.
7. Have a war outside with your friends.

Pronunciation Guide

cascarones	kahs-kah-roh-nays
Cinco de Mayo	sin-koh duh my-oh
Feliz Navidad	fay-lease nah-vee-dahd
Guadalupe	gwah-duh-loo-pay
piñata	pin-yah-tah
Posados	poh-sah-dohs
San Juan	san wahn

Words to Know

altar—table that holds holy things

ancestor—relative who came before

immigrant—person who comes to another country to settle

manger—box used for animal feed

solemn—very serious

Read More

Hoyt-Goldsmith, Diane. *Day of the Dead: A Mexican-American Celebration*. New York: Holiday House, 1994.

Marcus, Rebecca B. *Fiesta Time in Mexico*. Champaign, Ill.: Garrard Publishing, 1974.

Silverthorne, Elizabeth. *Fiesta! Mexico's Great Celebrations*. Brookfield, Conn.: The Millbrook Press, 1992.

Westridge Young Writers Workshop. *Kids Explore America's Hispanic Heritage*. Santa Fe, N.M.: John Muir Publications, 1992.

Useful Addresses and Internet Sites

Foundation for the Advancement of Hispanic Americans
6004 Roxbury Avenue
Springfield, VA 22152-1618

Hispanic Society of America
613 West 155th Street
New York, NY 10032

Hispanic Online
http://www.hisp.com/

Lent-Easter-The Ressurection
http://www.execpc.com/~tmuth/easter/

Index